V
E
R
N
A
L

VERNAL

poems

Kateri Kosek

Split Rock Press
2023

ISBN 978-1-7354839-6-2

Cover art by Aurelius Wendelken on Unsplash.
Book design and layout by Crystal S. Gibbins.

Split Rock Press is dedicated to publishing eco-friendly books that explore place, environment, and the relationship between humans and the natural world.

Environmental consciousness is important to us. This book is printed with chlorine-free ink and acid-free paper stock supplied by a Forest Stewardship Council certified provider. The paper stock is made from 30% post-consumer waste recycled material.

Split Rock Press Chapbook Series readers: Amy Clark, Crystal S. Gibbins, Whitney (Walters) Jacobson, Serenity Schoonover, and Natasha Pepperl.

www.splitrockreview.org/press

For Raphael Kosek,
poet and my mother

The other night, frogs crossed roads in the rain,
emerged from muddy dark & wet
into more of it,

following water down to where it seeps & holds—
the pools that won't stay long
but are here now, ready

for the stashes of jelly clear eggs,
the heady rush toward spring, its brief
cacophony.

We draw ourselves maps
as if we are not at every moment crossing
a thousand invisible paths.

It happens sometimes—the rain at night, the bodies
flattened under wheels.
Enough

of the eggs will grow heavy & fruitful,
clumped & hidden under leaves; floating
nurseries, black specks

of un-formed eyes. The pools will recede but even
in summer you can sense them, those hollows
where the damp comes first

& lingers dark in the leaves, where life was cached.

There is other evidence. Spring, the mud is heavy with tracks. On the road I walk between fresh plowed fields, the deep grooves of tractors. Beside them, tracking away from puddles: the soft swirled trails of earthworms—wandering, intersecting, not quite straight. They dry & harden in the morning sun, ancient etchings.

None of this is mine.

All the way home: my footprints in the mud.

Sometimes farm equipment rumbles down the road, sends up dust. But mostly the corn grows silent & unattended. So I help myself to these spring fields, the little road through them. Nights I can't sleep, I sprint down it if the moon is out. I learn not to apologize for what can't be helped.

The stashing of hopes in ephemeral pools.

How I think about you   thinking about kissing

the front of my hips.

Last year on the first day of spring, a flock of larks burst up from the middle of a cornfield. They arose from a place where the mud was showing through the hard, slick snow— brown blobs, the color of mud & corn stubble, so I hadn't seen them. They flew up with high-pitched, tinkling calls & landed again in the nearest patch of mud.

Last year, at the exact minute of the vernal equinox
                                        a flock of larks

                        materialized

    from the middle of a melting field
                        in a spot where spring   had breached

                        its muddy heart

& I took it as something good.

This year, I'm on my own.

I'm wary of thinking too clearly, of a path that isn't straight, taken in bounds. I'm wary of anything that doesn't threaten to fuck me up. The rain in the forest continues long after it is done,

        filtering down

                from the canopy

         dripping loudly down

   the leaves quivering.

Easter, I trespass through the empty fields at dawn. A thrasher singing in the half-light, the machines heavy & stilled. Deer tucked in the back fields, the rain puckering the river. The world waits every morning for us to find it. It feels possible we could be saved—from ourselves, from what we haven't

yet done.

I walk through the fields weeping, toward the river

weeping.

One evening, almost dark, a man hunting turkeys. *I'm just out walking*, I say, his car paused beside me. His cousin's land—doesn't usually let people on it. He mentions the turkeys, I assume, as a warning. Another day, a truck I don't see coming. The farmer. I point to the house—I walked here. I am looking at birds. I will go & stare at the river. I will cause no trouble here.

April is a quiet hush, a gift still unopened. The little leaves not yet burst out. We wake long before dawn, restless, weary. Is there one small gesture that won't consume us? The streams are all swollen & falling down the mountain. You've been trying for so long not to touch me.

Spring is still becoming & has time. Waterthrush. Pine warbler. The first ones are flirts, their songs lifting to cool woods, an empty stage. But they all come back so quickly. Soon, birdsong impossibly loud, their small bodies drowned in a profusion of blossoms.

Every year I forget.

I lean in a doorway, the wind rippling my clothes
around my frame & you mention this later—

        the doorway,

                        the wind,

        my frame.

We won't see a thing till the corn comes down.

The blackburnian warbler has a flaming orange throat,
sings a thin, buzzy almost-song high in treetops where
hemlock & pine darken the woods to a more
permanent shade. But I don't look up.

You can't see from here the fiery throats
or even the birds,
or how the top of the canopy
is flat & open as a field.

Later, there will be the tasseled shadows of corn, & the corn itself, the spaces between the neat dense rows, but there's nowhere to hide in an open field. In the woods, the pools—nothing to connect them that flows. They evaporate quickly, having no steady source or outlet.

What spaces shall we inhabit? I am not supposed to be here but please please don't make me leave.

I'm wary of a path that doesn't bend, of turning back once I've come this far. I look behind me, wary of getting caught. Sometimes I need to get lost, like that time in the woods at dusk when I kept going & missed the turn & then it was too dark to turn around.

A stream flowing black & silver. Steep banks.

Being stranded is nearly the same as being lost. I knew exactly where I was.

Sometimes you must stop moving, let the birds filter above you. If you wander from the trail, it is important to return to where you started. If seduced by the place where two streams join, dropping & gathering, sliding & gathering into impossible pools, it is important to go back the way you came. It is also important that you forget this at times.

Come fall, the muddy ruts will freeze solid

    & running in the dark, I will trip on them

      & my running will startle birds that have bedded down

(the thin cries of what I perceive to be larks, though of course

      I can't see them)

           & all the way home   I'll repent

      for displacing the sleeping birds

        for thinking I was alone here

              for assuming the ground

      would give under my weight

would spread

& take me in.

I reckon by the singing of birds, by what fades in & out. I clear myself trails so as not to get lost. We have no clear memory of our successes. Under logs I flip aside, sometimes, salamanders, their bodies black or blue-gray, shiny. Their roof lifted off, they bend & curl, naked in the light, the bright shock of the new. When this happens, I replace the log. It is not important.

We like to draw lines on our maps

we drive down our roads   at night in the rain

      have you noticed

at dawn

birds flop onto the back roads in the half-dark

           colorless and silent

    so different

from their diurnal selves

all form

    and movement   flash

      of underwing   they dart

from my headlights at the last

      half second   quick

      and pale

and careless

           I swerve

and brake   I don't know

    what they are

if they're drawn

    to the warmth

of pavement   to insects drawn

      by the warmth

or if   it's the open

                                        stretch of ground

                          a place to land

        where the light hits first.

How much do we allow ourselves

             I am good

     at slipping away   at taking things

            too far   I leap straight

for the water   unthinking

If there were a sweet hollow   filling

       with snowmelt

     where I might lay myself down

       If it weren't so late

   and raining

my footprints all over

             if they meant

we could find a way home.

ACKNOWLEDGMENTS

Heartfelt thanks to *Southern Poetry Review*, in which the opening section of this poem appears, entitled "Vernal."

ABOUT THE AUTHOR

Kateri Kosek is the author of *American Eclipse*, winner of the Three Mile Harbor Press Poetry Prize. Her poetry and essays have appeared in *Orion*, *Terrain*, *Catamaran*, *Creative Nonfiction*, *Briar Cliff Review*, and *Northern Woodlands Magazine*. She teaches college English and mentors in the MFA program at Western CT State University, where she earned an MFA. She has been a resident at the Kimmel Harding Nelson Center for the Arts and the Tallgrass Artist Residency in Kansas. She lives in the Berkshire mountains of western Massachusetts, and serves on the board of the Center for Northern Woodlands Education.

Made in the USA
Middletown, DE
25 September 2023

39324418R00019